Madama Butterfly

cal Score

WITHDRAWN

GIACOMO PUCCINI

DOVER PUBLICATIONS, INC.
Mineola, New York

Madama Butterfly in Full Score
is available in Dover edition 0-486-26345-2

Bibliographical Note

This Dover edition, first published in 2002, is an unabridged republication of the vocal score originally published by G. Ricordi, Milan, in 1906. Lists of credits, characters, and contents are newly added.

International Standard Book Number: 0-486-42203-8

Manufactured in the United States of America
Dover Publications, Inc., 31 East 2nd Street, Mineola, N.Y. 11501

MADAMA BUTTERFLY

Tragedia giapponese in two acts

Music by

Giacomo Puccini

Libretto by Giuseppe Giacosa and Luigi Illica after David Belasco's play
Madame Butterfly, itself based on John Luther Long's short story (1903).
Long's text was based partly on Pierre Loti's novel *Madame Chrysanthème* (1887).
English version by R. H. Elkin. Vocal score arranged by Carlo Carignani.

First performances

Original version: 17 February 1904 / Teatro alla Scala, Milan
Revised version: 28 May 1904 / Teatro Grande, Brescia
Definitive version (in a French translation): 28 December 1906 / Opéra Comique, Paris

CHARACTERS

Cio-Cio-San* [Madam Butterfly], *a 15-year-old geisha* . . . . Soprano

Suzuki, *her maid* . . . . Mezzo-soprano

B. F. Pinkerton,* *Lieutenant in the United States Navy* . . . . Tenor

Goro, *a marriage broker* . . . . Tenor

Prince Yamadori . . . . Tenor

Sharpless, *United States Consul at Nagasaki* . . . . Baritone

The Bonze ⎫
⎬ *Cio-Cio-San's uncles*   Bass
Yakuside ⎭   . . . . Bass

The Aunt . . . . Soprano

The Cousin . . . . Soprano

Cio-Cio-San's mother . . . . Mezzo-soprano

Kate Pinkerton, *the lieutenant's American wife* . . . . Mezzo-soprano

The Imperial Commissioner . . . . Bass

The Official Registrar . . . . Bass

Dolore ("Trouble"), *Cio-Cio-San's infant son by Pinkerton* . . . . *silent role*

Cio-Cio-San's relatives, friends and servants;
off-stage chorus of American sailors

Setting: Nagasaki, Japan, at the beginning of the 20th century

*Inconsistencies in the principals' names occur in Puccini's score as well as in standard reference works about this opera. Pinkerton's initials B. F.—for "Benjamin Franklin"—are reversed in the Italian text at their first appearance on p. 43 of this vocal score, "corrected" on p. 78, then reversed again on p. 161; Butterfly sings all three versions. (Elkin's English text is correct throughout.) Depending on which music edition or reference book one reads, Butterfly herself is identified as either *Cho-cho-san* or as the Italianized *Cio-cio-san.* The present edition retains the latter spelling of the original vocal score.

CONTENTS

ACT ONE

A Japanese house, terrace and garden
overlooking the bay, harbor and town of Nagasaki

ACT TWO
First Part
Inside Butterfly's house

ACT TWO
Second Part

END OF OPERA

Madama Butterfly
Vocal Score

Madama Butterfly
Vocal Score

Act I.

A Japanese house, terrace and garden.
Below, in the background, the bay, the harbour and the town of Nagasaki.

3

The curtain rises.

(From the room at the back of the

little house, Goro, with much bowing and scraping, leads in Pinkerton, and with much ostentation but

sempre stringendo

m.s.

still obsequiously, draws his attention to the details of the structure.   Goro makes a partition slide out

at the back, and explains its use to Pinkerton)

ritornando a tempo

Suzuki (still on her knees, but grown bolder, raises her head)

Your Honour deigns to smile? Your smile is fair as
Sor-ri-de Vostro O-no re? Il ri-so è frutto e

Suzuki

flow'rs. Thus spake the wise O-cu-na-ma: A smile conquers all, and defies ev'ry
fio-re. Disse il sa-vio Ocu-na-ma: dei cruc-ci la tra-ma smaglia il sor-

Suzuki

trou-ble.
-ri-so.

Suzuki **Poco meno**

Pearls may be won by smi-ling; Smiles can ope the por-tals of Pa-ra-
Schiude al-la per-la il gu-scio, a-pre all' uo-mo l'u-scio del Pa-ra-

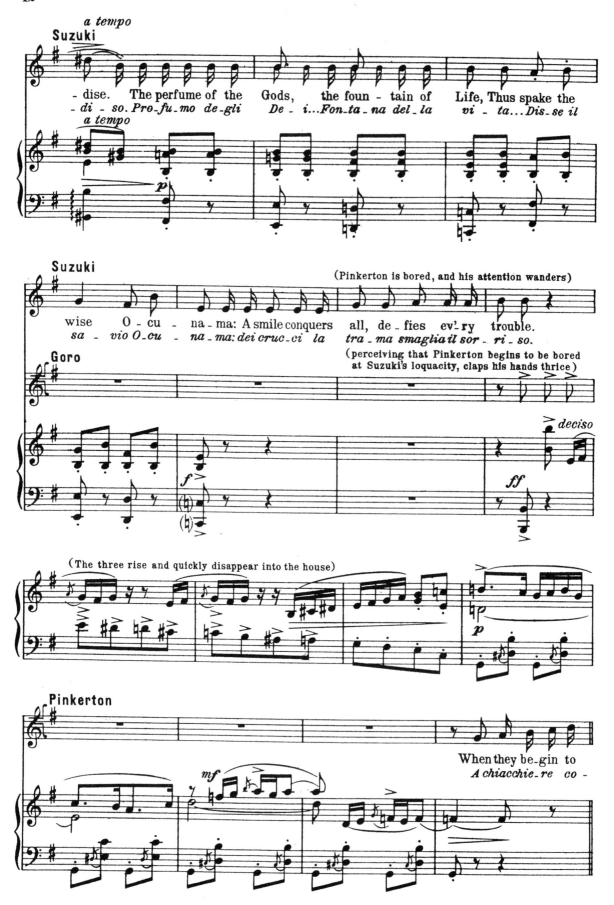

Goro
Here you'll sign the contract and solemnize the marriage.
Qui si firma l'atto e il matrimonio è fatto.

Pinkerton
Are there many relations?
E son molti i parenti?

Goro
leggierissimo
Her mother, grandam,
La suocera, la

Goro
and the Bonze, her uncle, (who'll hardly honour us with his ap-
nonna, lo zio Bonzo (che non ci degnerà di sua pre-

They bring glasses, bottles and two wicker lounges: they place the glasses and bottles on a small table;

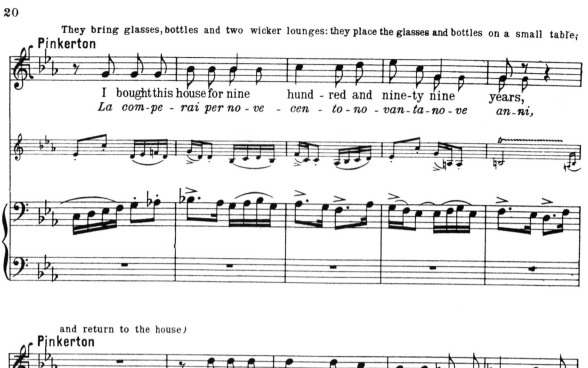

Pinkerton

I bought this house for nine hund-red and nine-ty nine years,
La com-pe - rai per no - ve - cen - to - no - van-ta-no - ve   an - ni,

and return to the house)

Pinkerton

but with the op - tion, at ev'-ry month, to can - cel the
con fa-col - tà,   o - gni me - se, di re - scin - de-re i

Pinkerton

con - tract!   I must   say,   in this coun-try,
pat - ti.   So - no in   que - sto pa - e - se

Pinkerton *a tempo*

maid.____
-mor.____

Sharpless *sostenendo*

A ve - ry ea - sy gos - pel which makes life ve - ry
è un fa - ci - le van - ge - lo che fa la vi - ta
dolce

p *a tempo* *p sostenendo*

Sharpless

pleas - ant, but is fa - tal in the end.____
va - ga ma che in - tri - sti - sce il cor.____

p cresc. e allarg.

Pinkerton **Iº Tempo.** *sostenendo*

Fate can - not crush him, he tries a - gain un - daunted.
Vin - to si tuf - fa, la sor - te rac - ciuf - fa.

f

Pinkerton

No one and no - thing breaks his pluck - y spi - rit. And so I'm
Il suo ta - len - to fa in o - gni do - ve. Co - sì mi

p

40

(Butterfly and her girl friends appear on the stage.
They all carry large bright-coloured sunshades open.)

50

Pinkerton

(Goro signs to the ser-

de - li - ca - cies that they fan-cy in Ja- -pan.
-bon-da lec-cor-nìa del-la Nip-po - ne- - rì-a,

vants to hurry into the house and to bring out everything)

(Having received fresh orders from Pinkerton, Goro is just going into the house himself,

when he perceives some more people climbing the hill; he goes to look, then runs to announce the

new arrivals to Pinkerton and Sharpless)

Pause.

ton has taken Sharpless by the arm, and leading him to one side, laughingly makes him look at the quaint group of relations.)

(The Imperial Commissioner and the official Registrar remain in the background.)

Pinkerton

What a farce is this pro -
Che bur - let - ta la sfi -

Pinkerton

Wood inst.

-cession Of my worth - y new re - la - tions,
- la - ta del - la no - va pa - ren - te - la,

Pinkerton

Held on terms of month - ly contract! (to Butterfly)
tol - tain pre - sti - to, a me - sa - ta.

Relations and friends

(4 only) Where is
Do -

60

68

bring out some small tables on which are placed various cakes, sweetmeats, wines, liquors and tea-sets.)

(They then place on one side some cushions and a table, with writing materials.)

72

76

84

88

(The friends cluster round Butterfly and congratulate her: meanwhile the Registrar removes the bond and the other papers, then informs the Commissioner that the ceremony is over.)

animando *rall.* *p*

Pinkerton

The Commissioner
a tempo (congratulating Pinkerton) *cresc. poco a poco*

The best of wish - - es.
Au - gu - ri mol - - ti.

a tempo

p *cresc poco a poco*

Pinkerton (bowing to him)

thank you most sin - cere - - ly.
miei rin - gra - zia - men - - ti.

p cresc.

Sharpless Sostenendo. *sempre cresc.*

The Commissioner I'll go
(approaches the Consul) *L'ac - com -*

May I ask, are you go - - ing?
Il Si - gnor Con - so - le scen - - de?

Sostenendo.

mf *sempre cresc.*

94

Pinkerton (to the child, giving him a lot of sweets)

Your turn, young ras - cal; spread out your hands and stuff up your sleeves
A te mar - moc - chio; spa - lan - ca le tue ma - ni - che insac - ca,

Pinkerton

(takes a glass and raises it)

With cakes and sweetmeats and lots of pas-try:
in - sac - ca chicche e pastic - ci a mac - ca.

Hip! Hip!
Ip! Ip!

Sopr.

(toasting)

Un poco meno, mollemente ♩ = 100.

Pinkerton

Let's drink to the new - ly mar - ried cou - ple,
Be - via - mo ai no - vis - si - mi le - ga - mi,

Yakusidé

Sopr.

Ka - mi! o Ka - mi!
Ka - mi! o Ka - mi!

Ten.

Un poco meno, mollemente ♩ = 100.

p marcato

sentito

96

98

(By degrees the voices grow faint in the distance. Butterfly remains motionless and silent, her face buried

in her hands, whilst Pinkerton has gone to the top of the path, to make sure that all these troublesome guests have really gone)

Butterfly (stoops to kiss Pinkerton's hand)

heart.

They tell me that a-broad, where the
M'han det - to che lag-giù fra la

cor.
Pinkerton (gently stopping her)

What's this? my hand?
Che fai?... la man?

dolce

pp

Butterfly

peo - ple are more cul - tured, this is a to - ken
gen - te co - stu-ma - ta è que-sto il se - gno

Butterfly

Un poco più mosso.

of the high-est hon - - our.
del mag-gior ri - spet - - to.

Suzuki (within) (murmuring)

And I - za - ghi and I - za - na - mi sa - run - da - si - co, and
E I - za - ghi ed I - za - na - mi sa - run - da - si - co, e

Un poco più mosso.

Suzuki

Ka - mi and I - za - ghi and I - za - na - mi sa - run - da - si - co, and
Ka - mi, e I - za - ghi ed I - za - na - mi sa - run - da - si - co, e

mf

Butterfly

(retires to a corner at the back, and assisted by Suzuki, carefully performs her toilet for the

Butterfly

night, exchanging her wedding-garment for one of pure white; then she sits down on a cushion and

Butterfly

looking in a small hand-mirror arranges her hair. Suzuki goes out)

I long to be rid of this pond-er-ous
Que-st'o-bi pom-po-sa di scio-glier mi

Butterfly

o - bi,... A bride must be robed in a
tar-da... si ve -sta la spo -sa di

Pinkerton (lounging on the wicker chair, watches Butterfly)

Just like a lit-tle squirrel are all her pret-ty movements! To
Con mo-ti di sco - jat-to-lo i nodial-len-ta e scioglie!.. Pen -

Butterfly
truth I must con - fess: At the be - gin - ning, all he said was use - less.
di - co in ve - ri - tà a tut - ta pri - ma le pro - po - se in - va - no.

Butterfly
A stranger from A - - merica! a
Un uo - mo a - me - ri - - ca - no! Un

Butterfly
for - eigner! a bar - barian! Forgive me, I did not know...
bar - ba - ro! u - na ve - spa! Scu - sa - te, non sa - pe - vo...

Pinkerton (encouraging her to go on)
My gen - tle dar - ling! and then? Con - tin - ue...
A - mor mio dol - ce! E poi?.. Rac - con - ta...

Andante mosso ma sostenendo ♩ = 84

con intenso sentimento   _entusiasmandosi_

Butterfly

But now, be - lov - èd,   You are the world,
A - des - so vo - i   sie - te per me...

Butterfly

more than the world to me.___ In - deed I liked you the ver - y first
l'oc - chio del fir - ma - men - to. E mi pia - ce - ste dal pri - mo mo -

Butterfly

mo - ment That I saw you.___
- men - to che vi ho ve - du - to.___

(Butterfly has a sudden panic and puts her hands to her ears, as though she still heard her relatives shouting; then she rallies and once more turns confidingly to Pinkerton.)

124

Pinkerton *(with ardour and embracing her affectionately)*
sostenendo

- cape. See, I have caught you... I hold you as you flut - - ter. Be
più Io t'ho gher - mi - ta... Ti ser - ro pal - pi - tan - - te. Sei

p sostenendo e cresc. *poco a poco*

Butterfly *(throwing herself into his arms)*

Yes, yours for e - ver.
Sì, per la vi - ta.

Pinkerton
allargando

mine. Come, then, come then....
mi - a. Vie - ni, vie - - ni...

f *b allargando* *mf*

Andante mosso appassionato ♪ = 120

Pinkerton *(Butterfly draws back, as though ashamed of having been too bold)*

Love, what fear holds you trem - bling. Have done with all mis -
Via dal-l'a - ni-ma in pe - - na l'an - go - - scia pa - u -

con anima

Pinkerton *(points to the starlit sky)* *Sostenendo*
con grande slancio f

- giv - ings. The night doth en - fold us!
- ro - sa È not - - te se - re - - na!
Sostenendo

con grande slancio
f

132

from the garden into the house).

The curtain falls. *dim. e rall.* — — — — — —

Act II.

Inside Butterfly's House.

FIRST PART.

Allegretto mosso ♩=144

The curtain rises: — The curtains are drawn, leaving the room in semi-

Sostenendo molto

darkness. Suzuki, coiled up before the image of Buddha, is praying. From time to time she rings the prayer-

-bell. Butterfly is standing rigid and motionless near a screen.

And I - za - ghi and I - za - na - mi Sa - run - da -
E I - za - ghi ed I - za - na - mi, Sa - run - da -

-si - co and Ka - mi   My head is throb-bing!   and thou,
-si - co e Ka - mi...   Oh! la mia te - sta!   E   tu

138

Lo stesso movimento

(acts the scene as though it were actually taking place)

Butterfly

rall. un poco

a man, A lit-tle speck in the dis-tance, Climb-ing the
un uo-mo, un pic-ciol pun-to s'av-via per la col-

Sostenendo molto.
Lo stesso movimento

Butterfly

hill-ock.__ Can you guess who it is? And when he's reach'd the
-li-na.__ Chi sa-rà? chi sa-rà? E co-me sa-rà

Butterfly

rall. **Lento.**

sum-mit, Can you guess what he'll say? He will call:"But-ter-fly" from the
giun-to che di-rà? che di-rà? Chia-me-rà But-ter-fly dal-la lon-

Butterfly

dis-tance. I, with-out answ'-ring, Hold my-self quiet-ly con-
-ta-na. Io sen-za dar ri-spo-sta me ne sta-rò na-

Andantino.

(Goro and Sharpless appear in the garden: Goro looks into the room, sees Butterfly through a

window and says to Sharpless who is following him:)

Goro.   **Allegretto mosso.**   (Goro and Sharpless

Come. She's here.
C'è.   En - tra - te.

cross the garden)

Sharpless.   (approaches and cautiously knocks at the door on the Right)

I   am   seek-ing...
Chie-do   scu - sa...

(doing the honours of the house)

(Butterfly invites the Consul to sit near the table: Sharpless drops awkwardly onto a cushion: Butterfly sits

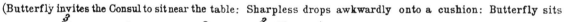

down on the other side and smiles slyly behind her fan, on seeing the Consul's discomfort: then with

158

Goro

She is poor as she can be.
El - la è po - ve - ra in can - na.
And all her
I suoi pa -

Goro

(Beyond the terrace the

re - la-tives have cast her off en - tire - ly.
-ren - ti l'han tut - ti rin - ne - ga - ta.

Prince Yamadori is seen, followed by two servants carrying flowers.)

Butterfly

(sees Yamadori and points him
out to Sharpless with a smile)

Here he is. Now list-en.
Ec - co - lo. At - ten - ti.

(Yamadori enters with great pomp from the door on the Right, followed by his two servants: Goro and Suzuki run up to him eagerly and go on their knees and hands before him. Then Suzuki takes the flowers and places them in various vases.)

(Yamadori greets the Consul, then bows most graciously to Butterfly. The two japanese servants having deposited the flowers, retire to the back, bowing deeply. Goro, servile and officious, places

a stool for Yamadori between Sharpless and Butterfly, and is very much in evidence during the conversation. Butterfly, Sharpless and Yamadori sit down.)

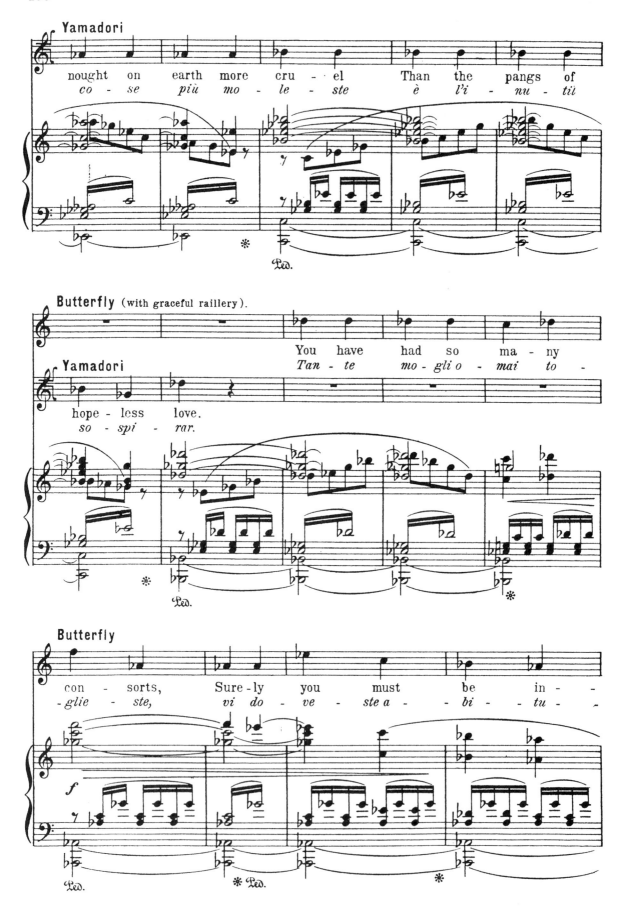

Butterfly

The pi-ty is: I will not...
Il gua-io è che non vo-glio...

Yamadori

would but...
- le - ste...

(Yamadori, after having bowed to Sharpless, goes off sighing; he turns again with his hands on his heart, cutting a

grotesque figure in the throes of love. The two servants follow him. Butterfly laughs again behind her fan and signs

to Suzuki to remove the tea. Suzuki obeys, then retires to the back of the room.) (Goro eagerly follows Yamadori.)

Sharpless

(Sharpless assumes a grave and serious aspect; with great respect, however, and some emotion, he invites Butterfly to be seated, and once more draws the letter from his pocket)

Un poco meno.

Sharpless

Now at last! Now if you please, be seat-ed here, And read this let-ter
Ora a noi. Se - de - te qui, leg - ger con me vo - le - te que-sta

(showing the letter)

Butterfly

(taking the letter)   (kissing it)   *poco rall.*   (placing it on her heart)

Show me.   On my lips,   on my
Da - te.   Sul - la boc - ca,   sul

Sharpless

through with me.
let - te - ra?

Butterfly   (to Sharpless, prettily)

sempre rall.

Andantino mosso. ♩=100
(gives back the letter and settles herself to listen with the greatest attention)

heart...   You're the best man that e - ver ex - ist - ed!   Be-gin, I
cuo - re...   Sie - te l'uo - mo mi - glio - re del mon - do.   In - co - min -

180

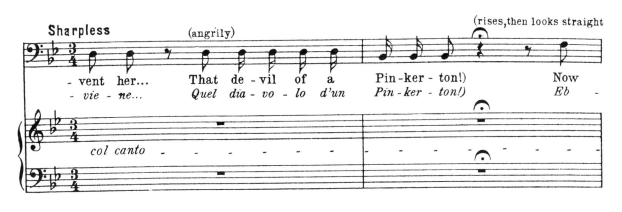

Sharpless *(angrily)* *(rises, then looks straight*

- vent her... That de-vil of a Pin-ker - ton!) Now
- vie - ne... Quel dia - vo - lo d'un Pin-ker - ton!) Eb

col canto

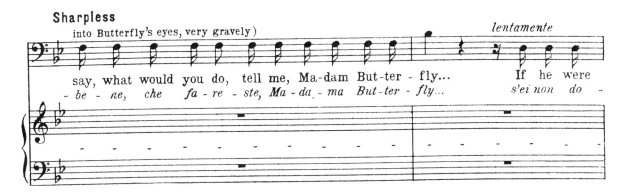

Sharpless
into Butterfly's eyes, very gravely)

say, what would you do, tell me, Ma-dam But-ter - fly... If he were
- be - ne, che fa - re - ste, Ma-da - ma But-ter - fly... s'ei non do -

lentamente

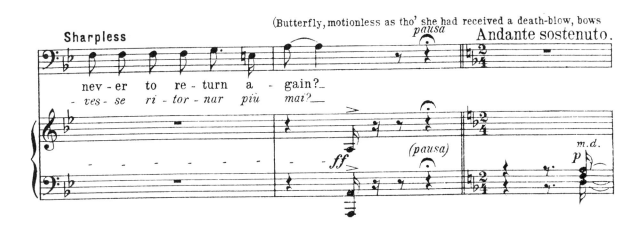

Sharpless

nev - er to re - turn a - gain?__
- ves - se ri - tor - nar più mai?__

(Butterfly, motionless as tho' she had received a death-blow, bows
pausa **Andante sostenuto.**

ff *(pausa)* *m.d.* *p*

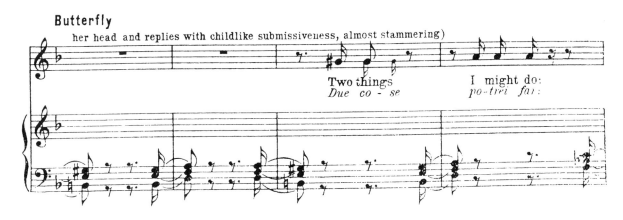

Butterfly
her head and replies with childlike submissiveness, almost stammering)

Two things I might do:
Due co - se po-trei far:

187

188

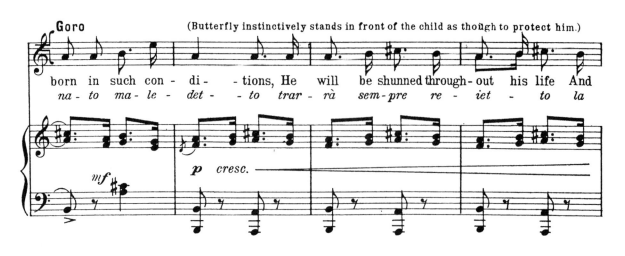

Goro

(Butterfly instinctively stands in front of the child as though to protect him.)

born in such con - di - - tions, He will be shunned through-out his life And
na - to ma - le - det - - to trar - rà sem - pre re - iet - to la

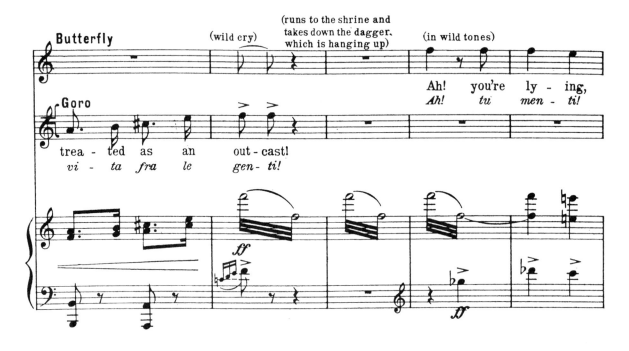

Butterfly

(wild cry)

(runs to the shrine and takes down the dagger. which is hanging up)

(in wild tones)

Ah! you're ly - ing,
Ah! tu men - ti!

Goro

trea - ted as an out - cast!
vi - ta fra le gen - ti!

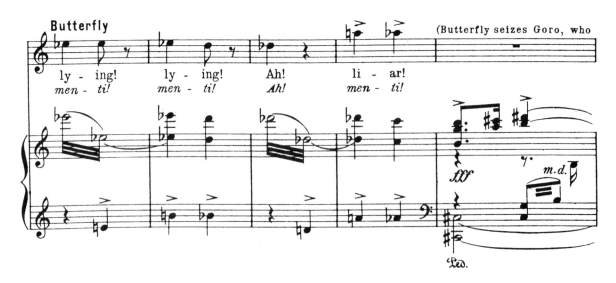

Butterfly

(Butterfly seizes Goro, who

ly - ing! ly - ing! Ah! li - ar!
men - ti! men - ti! Ah! men - ti!

falls down, and threatens to kill him. Goro utters loud, desperate and prolonged howls.)

Butterfly

Say't a - gain and I'll kill you!
Dì- lo an - co - ra e t'uc - ci - do!

Suzuki (thrusts herself between them; then horrified at such a scene, she takes the child and carries him into the room on the left)

No!
No!

calando e dim.

Butterfly (seized with disgust she pushes him away with her foot)

(Goro makes his escape)

Be - gone!
Va vi-a!

(Butterfly remains motionless as though petrified.)

204

212

Butterfly (taking the flowers from Suzuki's hands)

'Tis not e - nough yet.
Co - gli - ne an - co - ra.

(Butterfly distributes the flowers about the room, while Suzuki goes down into the garden again)

Suzuki (from the garden) **Un poco meno.**

How oft - en at this win - dow you've
So - ven - ti a que - sta sie - pe ve-

Suzuki a tempo

stood and wept and wait - ed, Gaz - ing and gaz - ing,
-ni - ste a ri - guar - da - re lun - gi, pian - gen - do

Butterfly

Suzuki

No more need I pray for,
Giun - se l'at - te - so,

in - to the wide, wide world beyond.
nel - la de - ser - ta im - men - si - tà.

lightly to and fro to the rhythm in a dance measure)

Butterfly
(Suzuki goes into the room on the left, and fetches out the baby whom she seats next to Butterfly;

ba - by.
bim-bo.

while the latter looks at herself
in a small hand-mirror and says
Butterfly   sadly)   rall.   Andante sostenuto ♩ = 52

How changed he'll find me!... Drawn wea - ry   mouth   from
Non   son   più quel - la!... Trop-pi so-spi - ri la

rall.

Butterfly

o - ver-much sighing, And poor ti - red eyes   from o-ver-much cry-ing!
boc-ca man - dò,....   e l'oc-chio ri-guar-dò____ nel lon-tan trop-po fi - so.

(throws herself on the ground, laying her head on Suzuki's feet)
Butterfly   (ardently)   cresc. _ _ _ (raises her

Su - zu - ki, make me pret - ty,   make me pret - ty,   make me
Su - zu - ki, fam - mi bel - la,   fam - mi bel - la,   fam - mi

cresc.   f   cresc.

Meno ♩=69

Butterfly (Suzuki closes the *shosi* at the back)

wait.___
-tar.___   (the night grows darker)

(Butterfly leads the baby to the *shosi*)

(Butterfly makes three holes in the *shosi:* one high up for herself, one lower down for Suzuki and a third lower still for the child whom she seats on a cushion, signing to him to look through his hole.   Suzuki

crouches down and also gazes out_ Butterfly stands in front of the highest hole and gazes through it remaining rigid and motionless as a statue: the baby, who is between his mother and Suzuki, peeps out curiously.)

Moderatamente mosso ♩ = 100

Sopranos

(humming)
(a bocca chiusa)

(within, from far off)

Tenors

(humming)
(a bocca chiusa)

(It is night, the rays of the moon light up the *shosi* from without)

Moderatamente mosso ♩ = 100

(The baby falls asleep, sinking down on his cushion;

Suzuki still in her crouching position, falls asleep too: Butterfly alone remains rigid and motionless).

(The curtain falls slowly)

✳✳ End of Act II
First Part.

Act II.
SECOND PART.

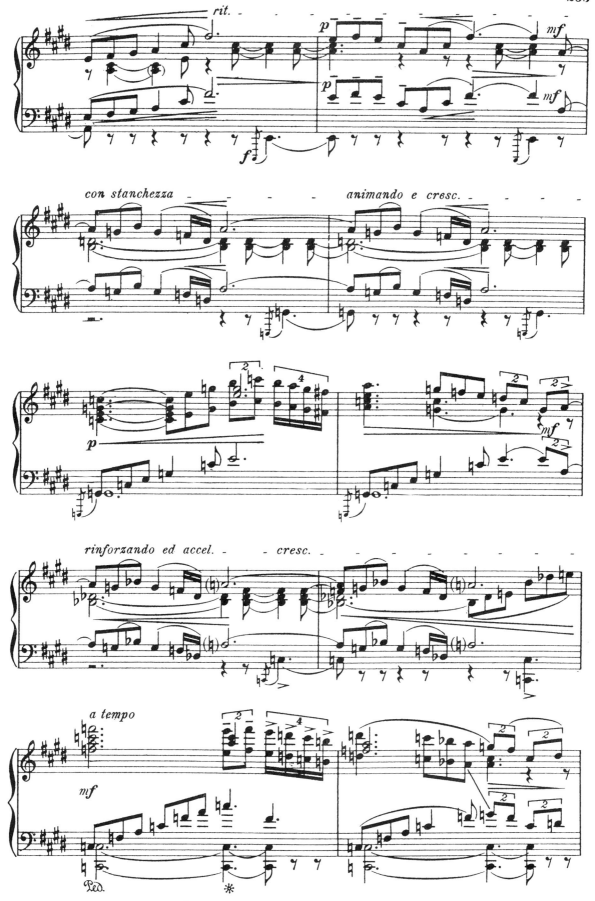

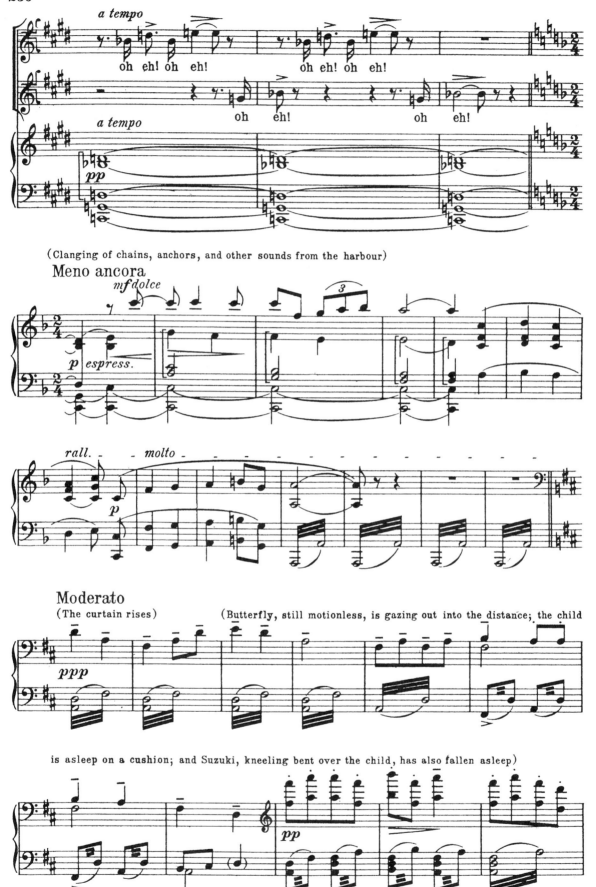

(Clanging of chains, anchors, and other sounds from the harbour)

Meno ancora

Moderato
(The curtain rises)   (Butterfly, still motionless, is gazing out into the distance; the child

is asleep on a cushion; and Suzuki, kneeling bent over the child, has also fallen asleep)

(The first streaks of dawn appear in the sky)

(The rosy dawn spreads)

(The day breaks).

(The sunshine streams in from outside)

242

Allegro agitato.

Pinkerton (giving Sharpless some money)

Give her this mo-ney, just to sup-port her... Re-morse and
Da - te - le vo - i qual-che soc-cor - - so... mi strug - go

Sharpless
told you?
det - to?

Allegro agitato.

Pinkerton
an - guish choke me, Re-morse and an - guish choke me.
dal ri - mor - - so, mi strug - go dal ri - mor - - so.

rall.

Sharpless
I warned you, you re - mem - ber? When in your hand she laid hers: "Be
Vel dis - si? vi ri - cor - da? quan - do la man vi die - de: «ba-

Sharpless
care-ful! For she be-lieves you." A - las! how true I spoke! Deaf to all en-
-da - te! El - la ci cre - de» e fui pro - fe - ta al - lor! Sor - da ai con-

260

262

Suzuki

Beats this lit - tle flut - ter-ing heart!
l'a - li bat - te il pic - co - lo cor!

(Butterfly gradually recovers; seeing that it is

broad daylight she disengages herself from Suzuki and says to her)

Butterfly

Too much light shines out -
Trop - pa lu ce è di

Butterfly

- side _____ And too much laugh - ing spring.
fuor, _____ e trop - pa pri - ma - ve - ra.

(The door on the left opens, showing Suzuki's arm pushing in the child towards his mother: he runs in with outstretched hands. Butterfly lets the dagger fall, darts towards the baby, and hugs and kisses

Allegro

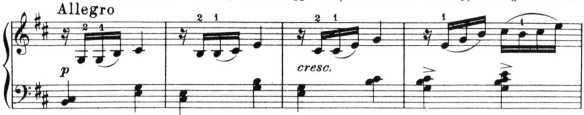

him almost to suffocation)

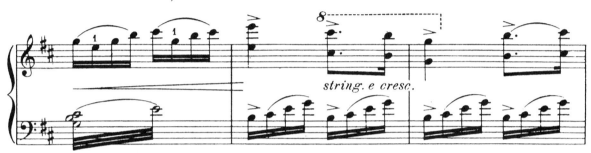

Butterfly

You? you?
Tu? tu?

secche

Butterfly

you? you? you? you? you?
tu? tu? tu? tu? tu?

ff